Heartsore

Po

Written & illustrated
by Anaïs Giulia
Edited by Tania Chick

Heartsong

Second edition 2023

Copyright © Anaïs Giulia

Illustrations © Anaïs Giulia

All rights reserved

No part of this publication may be reproduced without written permission from the author except for the use of brief quotations in a social media post, review or article.

Published by Flourishing Goddess, London

fallriseflourish.com

*Dedicated to my angel, my beautiful daughter Anna.
I love you.*

Contents

I On Life 1

II On Love 53

III On Magic 141

I

On Life

*"I have the right to say no
I have the right to not know
we are all sovereign beings."*

I Know

The smell of cinnamon
a warm place inside
a kiss on a rainy day
sweet oranges
a place in the woods
a garden full of flowers
the warm sun
the blue sea
the taste of your kisses
the scent of your skin.

One Good Deed

One good deed
is like a pebble in the sea
one grown seed
it grows in speed.

Auburn Trees

The sun shines through
I look at the sky and wonder
how many birds will I see today
smile to the sky
be grateful for what you have
cause every moment
it matters.

Violet Flower

The birds sing their song
in the treetops
they fly high in the sky
glowing light
the sky is blue with white clouds
enjoying the sun
life is so simple
at times.

Focus

Water train flies through the sky
in 1899 there were no planes
desert lands of golden sands
I collect myself
I just finished cleaning my house
I really like Sundays
I really want to travel
Vienna life bores me
the church bell sings
two candles burn
hello sunshine
where have you been hiding?
every thought and feeling
has its own magic.

Youthful

Cherry blossoms and a beach of white sands
make room for more laughter
champagne popping and cake to enjoy
dancing romantically
to the juice of sweet lemonade
let's go to the fun side
blue waters and green trees
many restful hours of sleep
reading books and learning new things
expecting miracles and love to come
the dance floor awaits.

Have You?

Have you seen the world of love?
the world of time?
spring summer
autumn winter
time
have you seen the world of hope?
south east west and north
the world is beautiful
from pole to pole.

Somewhere Called Home

Boil a soup
sweet tomatoes and sugar
rabbit meat and some potatoes
fresh warm bread and a rooster sound
flowers and butterflies
oven warm
a book in my hands
milk and honey
and some coffee
dog cats and birds in the garden
the world is big
a sleepy earthy place
the sun shines and glitters
the air is fresh and clear
maybe I will bake a cake
the mind of a woman
is the sweetness of Gods.

Sugar Cake

Let's make sugar cakes and plum roulade
kiss me softly and let me watch you smile
the world shines with you in it
crystal waters to be poured on us
time filled with passion and love
a kiss on the cheek
I close my eyes and dream of you
you are always welcomed in my world.

Milk With Honey

White whiskers
warm milk
eyes of wonder
smile on her face
the prettiest girl
l' amour
a blue chair
some blankets
two birds and a cat
having a cozy time.

Love is Red

The world is small
warm and sunny
my love for him is red
like cherries in the summer.

Fantasy World

Blue dress my girl wears
and sunshine in her eyes
red lips my lover has
red like the colour of wine
green eyes and a melody in her ears
she is a rare pearl
from the deepest ocean sea
beautiful inside and out
long hair my beloved has
and the prettiest of faces.

Today

The sea is beautiful
calm sunny day
the sky is blue and scented
like sugar cane.

Be Cool

The joy of existence
existence born of joy
peaceful moments
with you
warm hearts
lips to enjoy.

What?

Hear me say no to adventure
I am good where I am at
cause travellers are fools
to want or need to discover the world.

To be

Joy of being
flourishing and thriving
love is a wild jungle
full of plants and
budding flowers
the thrill of living
inside the story
the world around us
a star in the making
a flower blooming
the joy of existence.

Comfort Zone

Twilight zone
endless working hours
pondering on life
research is done
shift gears
to light
release strain and worry
will it pay off?
walking helps
sun therapy
watching movies
a change of environment
a different headspace
taking time for yourself
imagination
enjoy life more.

Love is Not a Fairytale

Cherries on trees
the sun loves the colour red
blossoms in gardens
the sun loves sweet perfume
of flowers
mountains take me high
towards the sky
trees tell me stories
of owls and foxes
insects and butterflies
the grass is soft and wet
the sea speaks of love
repeating wave by wave
love is not a fairytale.

Sandals on my Feet

Overworked
no interference
offers coming in
I don't want to jump right in
last minute
where to next?
this glorious world
pumpkin seeds and pears
I speak different languages.

Mother

Can one believe
in beauty
in desires and conquests?
I think my darling
dreams do come true
you are all what you request.

The Little Red Book

Dreams do come true
every day dream some more
works in the making
books to be read
boundaries to be set
my road
be careful with your steps
song of Isis
I tell my own story.

Be Aware

Illusions of truth
realness of dreams
gates wells and hills
to be open abandoned lived
wherever does the road lead to?
a time is needed for growth.

Worth Waiting For

Time is needed
for a seed to become a blossom
at the right time
under the right sun
it will blossom
as it knows
it needs only time.

Sovereign

The lens of paradigm
this reality doesn't define me
the past doesn't impress me
the future excites me
silenced echoes of shadow
intense ride
hurrah
I have arrived
learned my lessons and my sorrow
in my heart I know and will know
I am not going to change my mind
the road starts and
has always been there
take a step
let things be
I create
galaxies and the stars
it is my place to be
I have the right to say no
I have the right to not know
we are all sovereign beings.

Someone From the Past

The same paradigm
  does not compel me
time does not exist like we think
flowers are to be picked
new energies
step out
radical change.

Autumn

Trees have changed their colour
sunset orange sky
the night is cold
without him
wrapping me in his arms.

Checkmate

Don't take advantage of me
mermaid
infinity sign
fish and whales
I am not satisfied
so I've decided to abstain
I am no broken beauty
you are not your word
I am perfection
perfection that I am.

Don't go Back on Your Word

Keep your boundaries
strongly
keep it cool
your values
hold space
poker face
Lolita
sun moon rising
tenth house
I used to be brave
simply put
I don't care.

Lover of Poetry

Lover of poetry
fascinating mind
senses to enjoy
lover of words
delighting on love
the sun touches the sea
the stars shine in the sky
you see the world bright
flowers bloom in the grass
sea moves calmly
sun shines
the moon has quarters.

Spongebob

My work is valid
my hands create touch and feel
I will always protect myself
is it love or is it over?
baby don't hurt me
Pluto moon
I am a creatrix
when is the full moon?
it's my say
if it's meant to be.

Extraordinary

Dance moves
in opposition
I can walk and talk
several stories
simultaneously
do you know of another park?

Cherry

Images of paintings in my mind's eye
rose quartz
a bloomed tree and some fun
cherry is my favourite fruit
cherry blossoms
and orange ice.

Proserpina

Spring arrived
with happiness around it
my love is a flower
that never dies
it flourishes forever
in the garden of God.

Ode to Love

Heartbeat
a joyful feeling
love rides on the wings of a butterfly
towards the centre of the universe
melody of the heart
the world has uttered
words of love
and has tasted
happiness
on each others' lips
in each others' eyes
we have seen the truth.

The Cookie Carnival

Peace and tranquility
you don't faze me
overwhelmed
watering the seeds
have you seen drops of rain?
looking for good earth
give and take
letting go of people
how much do you love yourself?
it's a gradual process
be brave
for there is a reason for everything
bells of church
Saturday brunch
mentality shift
for the sake of me.

Home Again

As we sat on the grass
the rain starts
present past
you had joy in your eyes
and sorrow on your lips
why do we kiss?
sometimes things move too fast
or too slow
oasis of mind
a myth is a story
a story is a myth.

In the Zone

Miracles happen
love is true
beyond this tree
there is another one
and another tree
before the last one
torrent of rain
wet earth
a melody to remember
the good times.

Frightened

Feathers smoke
your eyes need time to reflect
my soul is broken
pieces to recollect
I am brave
an eagle to fly on
a pocket full of sand
and some salt
when you know that God is with you
all becomes clear
he shines his light on me
kisses my cheek
holds my hand
when you know you are loved
and you are love
no darkness can ever destroy that
3x3 makes nine
pray and rejoice
you are never alone
you needn't worry
God has a plan
for you are his creation
and his creation can only be good.

Child-like Innocence

Protect me my brother
be there always for me
protect me my sister
hold my hand
sweet petals.

Endless

The world is big and my love
will forever be
nothing is lost
or never seen
in the ocean of the heart
all is transparent.

Take it Easy

Manifestation poem
change
I don't want this to ever end
release of guilt
how do you know what pretty girls like?
tiger feline french chic
soft voice and gentle eyes
a box with a ring
who was the happiest girl in the world?
Marilyn Monroe
navy blue
anything goes.

Memory of Time

Pebbled streets
footsteps on the sidewalk
car lights
rush hour
memory lane
sweet lips
red wine
eyes on mine.

Yellow Brick Road

Follow the yellow brick road
   straight to the station
there I will await you with my luggage
to board the train together.

Emerald Love

Birds in the garden
sound of trickling water
green ferns
full of colourful flowers
butterflies and dragonflies
an orchard full of fruits
love is a garden
an ever-growing garden
protected by love.

Isolating Beauty

To dream like a boy
sadness in her eyes
everyone cheering
for the most beautiful girl
in the world.

Wise Woman

One day my love for him will cease
I pray to God he forgives
one day my love for him will (re)awaken
I pray I can forgive.

Pumpkin

Love is the art of lovers
a palpable feeling
touching
kissing
holding
eternally
stars and moons.

A Time to Remember

Have you felt her heartbeat?
have you kissed her lips?
do dreams fly as flies or butterflies?
the stars will align
dream on my butterfly
romanticism is not gone.

Water Lily

Crescent moon
golden eyes
evening sun
soft water
I dream of your eyes
in a beautiful garden.

Be Here With me

Where love begins
life never ends
love is a knot
of eternal time
whispered a thousand times
in the echo of my heart.

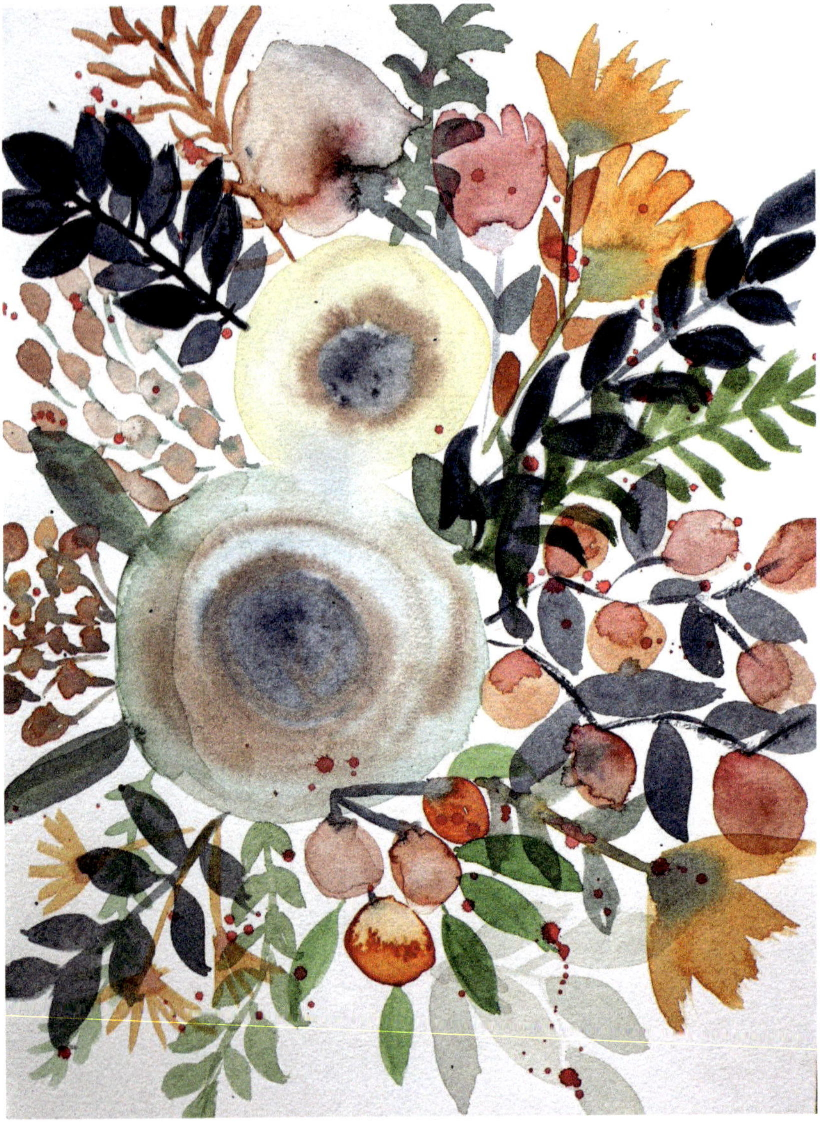

II

On Love

*"love doesn't burn out like a candle
and it doesn't wear out like sandals."*

Love of Mine

Shining light
of the moon
sweet love of mine
stars shine for you
the birds sing their song
to the world.

Blue Bird Sunshine Blues

Green is my love for you
my eyes see only blue
girl this thing called love
isn't easy to do
one evening my darling
the world is vibrant colours
strange pleasure
I just want your kiss
I'll be fine
I'll forever dance with you
the world is yet to see
my thrills with you
bowl of fire.

North Pole

I believe in you
magic unfolds
pleasure to be reborn
pleasure to be fulfilled
lips to be kissed
whispers in my ear
come closer to me
dazzling eyes
hear me saying
I am already yours.

Serenade

Ice-cream with jelly beans and a towel
I can get lost in you
the wind knows
you belong to me my friend
I'll do anything for you
my Greek God
you have the most beautiful eyes
the angels on our side
have allowed me to find you.

Here is my Hand

Call me your girl
be my boy
beloved of mine
sweet angel
hummingbird
most brilliant of colours
sipping nectar
from a flower.

Your Kisses Are Mine

euphoric laughter
behind your eyes
such sweetness
in your kisses
to have you near me
forever more
is a joy to behold.

Dream Girl Dream Boy

A walk in the woods
trees offer a home
soft green grass and earth
lay a blanket
dream girl dream boy
love is beautiful when it is shared
kiss my lips and close your eyes
a smile on your face
why can't we ever forget?
spectrum of light
the world is perfect
in your eyes.

Lipstick on my Lips

Baby I'm having fun
working with the sun
baby I feel good
in the winter
stellar gateway
I'll run away with you
you are my star crossed lover
when I am with you
I lose track of time
have you seen the ducks?
I just want to see you smile.

Happiness

Life awaits you
in the unknown
miracle one
miracle two
miracle three
oracle of life
emerald green eyes
red lips and big smiles
joy in your spirit
and love in your heart
kiss me once
and I will kiss you back
under the moonlight
our love will still shine.

Sunset and Sunrise

Hear me say yes to the unknown
don't tell me any stories
just give me your love
look me in my eyes
and tell me
if you've seen an angel
living on this planet
or if you've seen a love
more beautiful than ours.

Joy Giggles

Love sunshine
blue-petalled flowers
a flowing river
down the stream
joy is in our eyes
smiles and kisses
the world is beautiful
with you by my side.

It's a Good Day

Let's fly away to Las Vegas
June 25
Tom and Jerry cartoons
it's a good day to do whatever you please
there is nothing to lose being you
rise and shine
every day is a good day
from morning till night
to have some fun
it's a good day to be lazy
can you doodle?
I love you and you love me
let's fix it
you'll think I'm crazy
doing the doodles
boiling some noodles.

Lovers' Whispers

Boy meets girl
girl meets boy
that's how it all begun
one Saturday night
that's right
I fell in love with her smile
I met her on Monday
kissed her on Tuesday
met her family on Friday
took her dancing on Saturday
and we had an ice-cream on Sunday.

Hand in Hand

Hand in hand
lovely sunset
the sun sets slowly
because of you
the sea settled
sand in the sea
sand on the shore
because of me
birds sing in the sky
the world is a sweet cinnamon pie
when in love.

Morning Kisses

Petals on my bed
morning love
pretty eyes
my beloved has
pretty lips to kiss.

Good Vibration

When are you the happiest?
what things do you enjoy?
where is my Romeo?
hey Juliet
want to run away?
I know you really want me
you really blow my mind
I want to be your Romeo
let's go out dancing
a brand new dance
and a new chapter.

Red Dress

Ready to love?
can you see
how beautiful I am?
true eyes never tell lies
I love your mind
girl please be mine
the way you are and will be
together with me.

Blackbird

Take me home
hold my hand
lover of mine
I want to be with you forever
honey is the taste of my love
now that I have found you
the angels sing
up in the sky
love is beautiful
with you around
sing my melody
will you be mine?

Blossoms Pink Roses

The stars shine
let me stay with you
the sun warms
I am your lover
the rain clears and washes
would you like to be mine?
the night is the time of lovers.

Golden Stars

One golden star
was born a time ago
two golden stars
were born yesterday
my love for you
is as God loves me
eternally
forever more
endlessly you.

Sunshine

Your eyes are brown
my eyes are green
like the shades of a tree
the trees whisper to me
the flowers speak of spring
summer's in my heart
birds and butterflies.

Fascinating

Smile for me
it's marvellous
dance for me
my life is so glamorous
it's wonderful
how you care for me.

Forever Yours

In your arms I want to be
like a cocoon
with a thousand butterflies
in your arms I want to be
like a dream to unfold
every second of my existence
cherished
loved
protected
forever yours
I am.

Kissed and Sealed

Kissed and sealed
my love for you
king of heart
queen of your love
the sea doesn't know time
reaching the depth
my love is sealed
with your kiss.

Picture Perfect

Perfect you
perfect me
to love is to admire
meet me on a shore
and echoe to me
I love you
dream waters
dream love
my dream lover.

Make a Rainbow

Make a rainbow
of sun and rain
technicolour clouds
light the sky
green grass
some trees never die
moss and wet mushrooms
and a tent
fire sparkles in the sky
dance the night
and sleep the day
your love is my love.

Lover

My lover
makes me smile
he has brown eyes
makes me trust
my lover
has a good mind
makes me love
and love I do
he is my dream
come true.

Event

Imagination sparked
fusion of opposites
daydreaming
how many times does the sea wash ashore?
how many crabs are there on the sand floor?
how many wishes on the stars and trees?
how many ships left on the sea?
the rain pours and the sea hasn't ceased
what is scary?
nothing when I am with you
I've been holding onto a feeling
a feeling of love
holding on
what a sweet place to be
every time I see you
blue sea and wind on the seashore
water me down baby
wash my legs in water
smile sunshine.

Lovers' Whispers

Heart of mine
by your side I want to be
your kisses taste so sweet
violet blue petals
when the stars shine
I dream of you.

Kindred Spirits

Sweet pages
written on the shore
the sea is bright
the sun shines
trees are big and strong
shadow of the moon
shining of the sun
heart to heart
hand in hand
our love shines bright
under the sun.

Imago

The sea speaks to me
the sky watches me
you are my lucky star
understand that
my eyes are blue
your eyes are black
where the wind blows
I trust I will find you
the sea will embrace us and
tell us all of its secrets
the world doesn't end
but it begins with you.

Eternal Love

Castle on the wind of life
flying in the sky high above
sweet delight
hear me say
I've known you before
in another lifetime
you and I
were lovers
I have promised you forever
so here I am
once again in your arms
after crossing the galaxy of time
ever lasting
ever joyful
ever loving
is my love for you.

Garden Water

Garden water
Grays of sunshine
my beloved in my arms
rose water
flower petals
my beloved in my arms
sky of wonder
stars of God
my beloved in my arms.

Purple Rain

Time upon time
desert lands
drinks of ocean
on the shore
cool nights
a tent and a fire
love doesn't burn out like a candle
and it doesn't wear out like sandals
fields and fields of blossoms
I never want this to end
fish in the sea
birds in the sky
blossoms to open
behind a tree there is a spot
it's called purple sex
rain and rain
the sky is blue
and the air is clear
where do the angels meet?
time tells a story without an end
ripe apple and orange trees
sweet delight and roses.

Embraced

Past present future embraced in one kiss
hold my hand and dance with me in the waters of time
cause God made us beautiful
kiss me sweet and we will smile together
the water is warm and there are trees on the shore
past present future embraced in one love
nothing is more beautiful than life itself
and heaven awaits the lovers
time never goes by
without to kiss
the moon is round
the stars shining make me think of your eyes
and your eyes make me think of your smile
come closer to me lover
and hold me in your arms
we will spend this life together
holding the love of a lifetime.

As Flowers Unfold

Petal by petal
shade by shade
colour by colour
gently softly tightly
rays of sunshine
watery gardens
drink my beloved in
from these beautiful blossoms
ready to reveal
the essence of a flower
rain petals
sweetness wetness
purple and black
smell of heaven
it takes a while to see
the beauty of a flower
senses to arise
one by one and simultaneously.

Behind me

You wrap me up in gold
you see the world
piano time
my muse
lipstick and romantic places
why hurry when you can enjoy?
the tenderness of your cheek
remembering the beauty of us
my love is an elephant
nights of passion and tenderness
remember what you have
lovers love your smile today
the dreams you know are true
lovers will come and go
like the wind
ride those waves
ride those roads
go to what you love.

Yellow Bird

Blue mountain
yellow fountain
flower water
watermelon
love is a moon to be kissed
and a sun to bathe in.

Tell me

Tell me a story of love
message in a bottle
over the sea
finding its way to me
tell me a story of a happy time
share with me the heart of wonder
shore of water
sea of foam
I'm happiest with my love
waters are blue
the sun shines through
warm is my love for you.

Blue Crystal

Seaside love
breath in slow
love on a shore
not alone
the world is big
and I will see it
the world is beautiful
and I will enjoy it
deep blue crystal
deep blue dream
dreams do come true
when you find love
and love finds you.

Perfect

A life with you
sweetheart of mine
your words my word
green eyes my lover has
yellow petals
sweet delight
snow clouds
a yellow tree
I have searched for you
you have found me
your love is king
be mine forever.

Ocean Eyes

Like the ocean with her power
moving the earth
so is my love for you
like trees growing green
their roots inside the earth
so is my ache for you.

My Wonder

Love is miraculous
a God-given wonder
unity in the making
a beautiful tale
the sea
the sun
shining on us
a midsummer's evening
beautiful people
love is a realised dream
with you.

Loved

Sun kissed
moon loved
which land is mine?
green love
green luck
I will tell you the truth
because time is the truth-teller
show me your love
I'll show you mine
or vice-versa.

Heart to Heart

Heart to heart
the lover whispers my name
heart to heart
sweet sound of your voice
calling me
in your arms I want to be
one kiss and then a thousand
pressed on your lips
my love has a name
of flowers and sweetness
in the air.

Forever

History untold
on the sea forgotten
the story has no end
it goes on forever
the miracle to come
cherished my love
for me and you always.

My Golden Star

The world is blue
and full of magic
ocean waves
washing ashore
love is a waterfall
crossing the mountains
falling into the sea
swiftly.

Dancer

Swirl of music
slow orchestra
dance of lovers
four hands kissed and touched
who doesn't love a man unafraid to love?
some kisses are not to be told!
my hands your hands
like lovers do
when we are happy
God smiles upon us
tap dancer step by step
a black crow
shadow dancer
choose your song
generosity is what makes you good
happiness is contagious
God given gifts
long hair
time to be happy
dream big
adventure is to follow
balance and grace
ease and beauty.

Feel me

Our kisses never end
your eyes make me
dream again and again
my love
there is beauty in you
I want to see it all
kiss me again and again
seeing your eyes
there is no secret
you are my Valentine
your love feels
like a dream come true
darling
to me
you are the most beautiful.

Shining Stars

Love is beauty
beauty is love
a shimmer blue sea
stars in the sky
a golden sun
a beautiful garden
shining stars
love is us
wrapped eternally
in the arms of God.

Jazz Vibes on

Where is my Valentine?
I've been missing him
he never comes to hear me say
mr. Valentine
trumpets sound
would you have this dance?
slow touch
my mr. Valentine went missing
can somebody please tell me where he is?
my funny Valentine
wait for him to come
the songs of laughter
are still to be sung
my mr. Valentine
loves to sing for me
he is humorous
and makes me laugh
he knows I'm his girl
I know he will be there
wishing for more
but who knows?
I'm his red ruby.

Shimmer Blue Sea

Shimmer blue sea
clouds as shade
the sun comes and goes
I start to wonder
once dark once light
the birds fly high
shades of the sun
clouds soft and white
this boat sails to new lands
shimmer blue sea
have you seen my lover?
he is gone missing
shimmer blue sea
have you seen my lover?
I'm searching for him.

Let's do Something Fun

His eyes oh my
I watch him so sadly
I want him so badly
oh my poor heart
how can I tell him that I love him?
young and handsome
but he doesn't see me
turquoise green.

Conquest

When I think of him
white petals conquer my heart
white yellow flowers
the sunshine believes
happiness is foolish dreams
fly away
come back to me
wind blows
trees fold
cherry is the colour of my lips
your eyes my beloved
make me wonder
your lips my beloved
dream of me.

Desire me Always

Red polished nails
old vintage books
and a blue door
Jack's market
a street corner
a man buying ice-cream
a lovely summer's day
the time has come to wonder
seeing the city from high above
you old crazy moon
what did you do?
look what you've done
sending my lover away
unbreak my heart
old crazy moon…

Moon Waters

Who I am to judge or be judged?
water of rivers flow
behold the tree
there is a light
I hold it in time
the light of hope of love to be
to trust to see
what is unfolding
holy at my chest I hold
I see I breath I touch I feel
like pandas in the night
moon kiss.

In my Heart

My beloved in my arms
as time has stopped
forgetting who we were
just thinking what we are
wishing to stop time
or rewind
and let this moment last forever
cause what has passed
is never lost
it tends to live on forever
in my heart.

Lips to Kiss and Eyes to Dream

Your love is my medicine
the one that cures every shadow in my heart
your love is sweet honey
that nourishes my soul
your kisses taste like the fruits of heaven
your eyes open every door in my heart
living a dream
of true love.

Cradle of Love

God has made you
out of love skies and stars
clouds of white
when you were born
the world sang
sweet love of mine
having you in my arms
is heaven on Earth.

Unchained

I feel like a misty song I hear
little things bring me happiness
a cigarette red lipstick and an address
my heart swings for you
funny thing
I want to give up on love
but my heart won't let me
everything still reminds me of you
what can I do?
are you coming to me or not?
I guess I'll just call a cab
and wait for you at my place
candle lights on my corner table
how lucky am I to have met you?
thinking of our times
and the beauty that is spring.

Blessed be

Inside you I find a heart to keep
inside me I feel a surge of a wave
cause love is not a fairytale
and love is not a cube with colours
love is being with one another
that's how love feels
through us my love
a never-ending story.

Because of You

Because of you my beloved
my life is beautiful
because of you my lover
my heart sings of happiness
because you
my love flourishes even more
my beauty shines
the world is beautiful
with you by my side.

Last Chapter

A book without end
pomegranate
timeless women
fill an empty space
wrap me in your arms
lily of the valley
smell me white
he loves me he loves me not
petals to be told.

Salt Water

My heart is not like the wind
or like the waters
my heart is a stone
of galactic wonders
follow the wave
start middle end
of what to be become and
never was to be.

Blue Moon

The world hasn't seen a love like this
the birds sing
the moon swings
my love for you
makes an entire world
the world hasn't seen a love like this
deep as the ocean
strong like a waterfall
when we kiss
the entire world sings.

New Dawn

Seal my heart with honey
let it drip bit by bit
sweetest pleasure
of a heart left to bleed
let your light shine through the darkness
that has closed your soul
let yourself taste the sweetness
of your immortal soul
let no more sorrow be
no more sadness nor defeat
let the morning come
and you shall smile with it
a new dawn every single day
to bring you closer
to where you need to be.

Dream Away my Lover

The time has changed
I am sorry beloved
I'm terrible at love
I'm sorry if I disappoint
I have to say goodbye
please forgive me but I have to fly
free like the bird of paradise
I'll wait you at our place
I know you will miss me
but I will be there to protect
I know we will meet again
9 o'clock at the cathedral of St. Paul
bittersweet song
meet me there.

Cry For me

I cheated love
by naming it
a gift from Cupid
when it is indeed a gift
from Aphrodite
an emerald stone
beauty has a name
called love.

Traces of Memory

Lines to be traced on my heart
roads we have been on
glimpses of a past and what is not forgotten
dreams of a distant place and how it felt
what brought me here is
what is going to bring me home
like a whistle to be blown
I miss you my friend.

Come Back to me

Long awaited lover
the land is vast
the ships are returning
one will bring you back to me
long awaited lover
the sea is big
my heart even bigger
I'll sing to the sea
every day my lullaby.

Together

Two days have passed
no letter
no word
no ocean.

The Ocean Speaks to me

Promise me
 you will always be near
the ocean speaks to me
telling me of you
seashells whisper to me
telling me you are mine
mine to have
forever yours.

White Petals

White petals
my melody doesn't end here
kiss my dreams away
together is what we have.

Never Leave me

Inside the letter
a rose lies
what you keep inside
my love for you never dies.

Lover's Dream

The sea is wild
like a lover's dream
to wash away
come back again
love is a butterfly
living eternally
on the wings of time.

Blessed be You Heart Keeper

The heart that loves more than it bears
love of kindness and integrity
love for God and one's country
besides this there is one word
free
free the bird.

Heart

Two days have passed
and no sight of him
the world has neither stopped
nor begun.

Back to You

These stairs will bring me back to you
straight into your arms
an empty station
back in time
waiting for my line
how many foolish things have I done for love?
and still my heart calls for you
the scent of roses and the clouds are gone
boo boo how strange love is
at times
your kisses are still made for me
you will not forget
the way of lovers like dreamers
when you are gone I lose my mind
for you.

Forever With me

Just a room full of books
a letter on the table
your words
I miss you
my love.

Melody For You

No one will remember
but I will
until we all fall down
show me the way
because I am down
never feel your ashes
until we meet again my friend.

On a Shore Alone

Meet me on a shore alone
we will search for pebbles on the sea shore
and leave our footprints in the sands of time
smiling once more hand in hand
we will walk
where to my love?
will you lead the way?
open your hands.

Are You Crazy or a Fool in Love For me?

To want to love is a risky game
like swimming above the sea
darling don't be difficult
the devil smiles
tired of games
promises are gone
time and time again
you try to find me
the light needs some shade
these wooden trees
don't keep forever
the dreams
their roots to be formed
the piano plays
and I feel alone
are you even real?

Sunday Dance of Sadness

Human heart
love affairs
baby I'm a fool
look me in the eyes
hear my heart beating
the sea is big and dangerous
but through my hands love flies above
when the bed is empty and my hands are busy
does my love do you any good?
only my love holds the flame
afraid of snakes
will you ever come back?
does it hurt?
don't say goodbye to my love
the entire world stings
come back to me darling.

Love Bubble

I love all of your colours
your shades and your mistakes
the things that hurt
are things to love once again
love always brings you back home
no matter how big the hurt
love again.

Magic Unfolding

Dream my lover
of a distant land of sorrow
inside your desert land
of high trees and rainbows
unicorns and magic
dream of you and me together
of a future hand in hand
dream my lover of nights full of passion
of sweetness and spectacle
and a softness in my voice
dream of lands of happy people
and a never-ending unfolding story.

Together

Inside the story
many stories live
one forever mine
one forever yours.

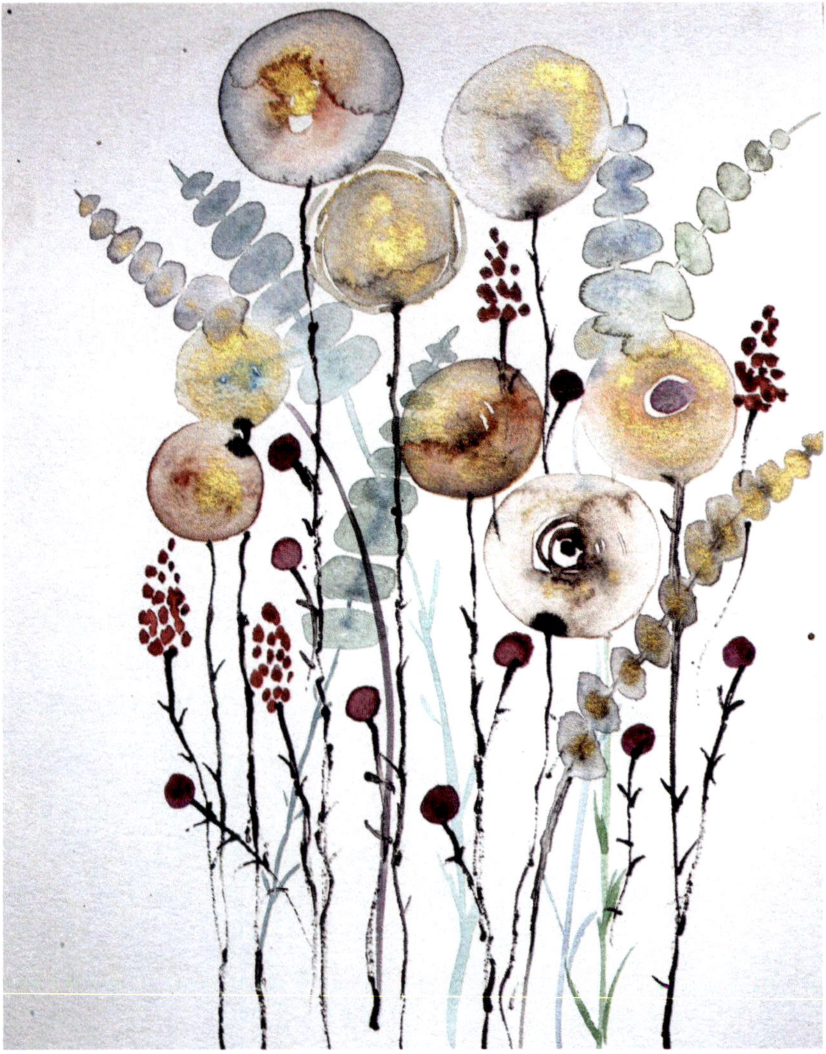

III

On Magic

*"darling never mind
these wings of yours
are the beauties of infinite time
life is a glimpse of the divine."*

Lovers

Lovers and the moon
creators of stories
anew ideas
past lives
psychic talents
keep it light
feel in balance
moonlight
the hermit
too much quarrel
simplify things
long term
walking card
the chariot.

Fairytale

Inside my story
one to be told
one to be cherished
one to blossom
as roses unfold
their rose petals
my love for you
is a sweet flower.

Moon Sunshine

Moon sunshine
stars twinkle many a time
to watch the sky
petrol-blue night
moon whisper
love me
love me
love me
say you'll be mine
whisper dream
moon shines her light on me
dream of me
the stars shine beautifully
like your eyes.

The Moon

The moon
makes me dream
of something beautiful
the stars are bright
shine on me your light
tell me you love me
like your child
dear moon
hear my wishes
fulfil my dreams
moon of love
moon of dreams
moon of light
the blue is bluest
when you are around.

Aphrodite

You shine more than the sun
the bluest of blues
the greenest of greens
red is the colour of love
your voice sings a birdsong
beauty is your entire essence
no one can look away
once they see you
forever charmed
lovers pray to you
lovers crave you
lovers dream of you
night and day
the sky dreams of your beauty
the stars wish to touch you
the earth loves you.

The Firefly

Soft angelic voice
like the sea
sing a little tune
let my heart enchant your eyes
and see how much I love you
do you hear that soft song?
have you dreamt of something new?
blue birds in the moonlight
night owl in the day time
my heart says hoot hoot
are you to be mine?
that's how I feel with you
blue birds dancing a little song
those blue birds
singing a tune.

Sirens

Dream my kisses
dream my love
the sea is big and dangerous
love keeps me safe
the stars guide me
the sun warms me
love the sea
love the mountains
love the birds
the sea is a love
that gives me a home
big and cold is its waters
beautiful sea
hear my melody
beautiful sea
bring my lover back to me.

Sky and Stars

Sky and stars on the dark sky
shining lightly above us
the big round moon
guiding our steps
the sea has whispered
love is my world
the night is sparkling
the sun asleep
the moon rays
gently touching
our love is calm
in the moon night
silver light.

Sands of Time

Heaven wisdom
orchards of oranges
we sat on the grass and had an ice
bubblegum
I could see the sea from there
sparkly in the sun
why is everything so beautiful and painful at the same time?
why can one not coexist without the other?
the colour of my eyes
green emerald
water and rain
sun and light
the dance of the moon
like the seashore
or a heartbeat
on planet Earth
everything that is beautiful has to be protected at all times
we are sacred in God's eyes
we are safe in his hands
two kids are playing in the sand.

The Garden

Rose petals
flowers smell sweet
breathe in the wonder
wet leaves and dark
blue sky
white clouds
softness in the air
my word is honey
bees and butterflies
dragonfly
blue and green
emerald black lines.

Queen of Hearts

Water ocean
sea of foam
wash me whole
moonlight on my shoulder
gateway of love
orange warm sky
the sun sets
the arms of my lover
touching me sweetly
namaste
a place to lay my head down
white and blue doves
rush me not
let me feel free
can we be real?
pancakes for breakfast
flowers in my hands
water fire earth and air
nature unfolds
roses smell
like heaven
blue is my favourite colour.

Sirens in the Water

The world is beautiful
the sea is deep
a curious mind
turquoise waters
blue sky
the world is green
and blue its waters
kisses are the lovers quest
touching hands
and smiles to share
lovers love the moon
bright and shining.

Poseidon

Lover of the sea
great King
your story began a long time ago
when God created the world
he made you King of the Nymphs
to rule the sea
and keep its secrets
lord of the sea
your wild spirit
is softened by your tender heart.

Sailor Neptune

Dark night sky
upon the horizon
the sun warms
the cold night away
Neptune
ruler of the sea
dark and bold
oceanic giant
aquamarine waters
made of stardust
golden light
and blue wonders.

Aphrodite II

essence of love
beauty of the world
the sun shines
and brightens your beauty
immortal Goddess of love
the sea has spoken
your eyes dream love
Aphrodite is your name
Poseidon your father
Aphrodite beautiful goddess
the poets dream life
and write sonnets
for you.

Flowers Bloom

Flowers bloom each and every spring
never dwell on the past
life is here for you
don't pass up on it
beneath the earth water flows
believe the stars are real
and twinkle in the darkness.

Float on

Seeds in a basket
fixed sign
cold and dry
being comfortable in letting go
good trips
in alignment
lighter steps
good space
to be understood.

Unstuck

Weekly practice
balance report
spaceship room
undisturbed space
independent
stepping out
grounding
shifting my vibe
I live a lot in my mind
invitation to have fun
need to speak with friends
have the opportunity
to have fun times
the wheel of fortune
crow spirit.

Saturday Evening Fun

Got to have a little fun
dance the night away
some sparkle and some gold
got to shake those legs
the music is calling
some fellows like singing in the rain
and wish for the sun to come through
let's have the time of our lives
dance the night away
sing throughout the day
smile and drink some champagne
let your worries fade away
we are young and ageless.

Protected

Sea mountains and birds fly high
green tourmaline
red earth and flowers in the sun
unity of love
fruits of heaven
river of afterlife
breaking free
of the past
the sun softly warms my eyes
and my smile warms every heart
shining light
clean air and the scent of summer
all that's empty will be fulfilled
butterflies
bees and birds
trees green and big
may love always be with you
sands of time
many doors
some open
some remain closed
don't shy away
life is what one makes
when one loves
stay true to your love.

Moonlight

Pyramids of sand
memories of the past
clear the air of dust
embrace life
rainbow in the sky
the truth is not in the middle
nor at the end
it is at the beginning
past present future
one seed two seeds three seeds
multiplied by a thousand
eons of time
miracles of life
unfolding in time
past present future
embraced in one kiss.

Guidance

The child knows everything
a tree has many seasons
to lose and to gain
is synonymous
to read the past
see into the future
let your heart guide you.

Little Flows

Little flows
little reach
water breach
softly moving
calming crystals spread
up and down the valley
little stones
little waves
fish swim
spring water
crystal clear
softly brushes
on the earth
beautiful water
moon love
sun warm
blue sky
birds in the air
fish in the sea
love is all there is to be.

Mermaid Song

Crystal blue our water is
warm at the surface
cold in the deep
deep blue sea
hear my melody
the land is vast
and its waters bigger
rays of sunshine
rainbow in the sky
the sky is soft and white
my beloved is in my arms.

Wonder

Why is the world red and blue?
why is the world green and yellow?
why is the sun yellow and the sea blue?
why are my eyes green?
why is red the colour of love?

Mermaids

Do mermaids fall in love?
does their heart seek the beloved?
are their lips kissed?
water blue waters
do mermaids have black hair?
do they enjoy the sun during the day?
water blue waters
do mermaids even exist?
water blue waters
I find mermaids
fascinating.

Behind the Trees

Glitter footsteps
above the water
green grass and trees
yellow sun
warmth in the clouds
beyond this sky
there is another one
with the same stars
a moon that shines
blue whispers
silence moves around in circles.

Distant Space

Hindering heights
mountains out of reach
planets stars and seasons
shadow moon
bright moon
red moon
wolf moon
water ebbs and flows
to wash ashore
all that is not pure
to be no more.

Sirens Magic

Long river
deep sea
ocean water
lake water
salt water
sweet water
sirens magic.

Believe in me

Mermaids of the past
and the ocean vast
stars in the sky
the beautiful sea
that brings my lover to me
to kiss
to hold
and tell him I love him.

Lovers Love the Moon

Lovers love the moon
shining in the sky
evening time
sweetness is in the air
cusp of summer
birds in the air
lovers love the moon
a kiss a smile a dream
of summer.

Ancient Kemetic

echoes of a long lost time
high mountains and windy cliffs
no one in sight
the land is vast
and it echoes in time
the sea is bright and shallow
the bluest of waters
golden is the colour of love
time stands still and is
our most merciful God
life moves still with grace
proud and eternal mind
how can we get in touch with God?
rest assured
God has a plan.

Quests

Be assured the sea is blue
and dark at night
dangerous and beautiful
at the same time
river sea and ocean
all stars shine
behind the horizon you'll find
red and orange colours
the sea is big
oceans vaster still
rivers flow
between the mountains
the sea beneath the earth
caves and secret places
under the sea
quest and quests
to be opened
to be closed
behind this horizon the world is big
earth water air and fire
all creating Earth.

Oracle of Dreams

Strength and faith to rule my way
growth and rain to nourish
and a heartbeat to follow
a cave for safety
and dreams to fly
are you scared of the truth?
are you brave enough to know it?
will it make your blood boil?
one plus one makes two
mother of witches
bringer of storms
are you here to learn my friend?
the deeper the cave
the longer the way
a bottle of wine
and good times to come
a miracle or two
a gift and a wise word
we are all here to learn
will you enter the doors?
mother of witches
help me with my wishes
queen of the underworld
blessed be forever
you will return.

What is Beautiful in the World

A chest of money
gold and jewellery
pirate band
the elves know the secrets
they appear at doors and trees
and at the riverside
they hold the miracle of wellbeing
and can accept wishes
they know stories upon stories
to other worlds of time
past present future
intertwine
a magical blade
a ship on the sea
with stars alight
night sky with a waxing moon
when all is quiet all is well
hear the breath of electricity in the air
one can only wonder and not despair
at sea one hopes for the best.

Pirates Journey

Wild sea
pirates are brave souls
they leave the world
to follow their dreams
new lands to seek
magicians of the sea
the ocean knows their stories
their battles and conquests
their ship is sailing
following the stars in the sky
towards the heart of the Earth
they seek adventure
pirate ship sailing to new lands
to conquer their waters
guided by the stars
their heart is wild
wild as the sea
pirates are brave souls
wanting to conquer
the world.

Heart of Magic

Heart of magic
heart of love
gilded treasure
of a life to come
pleasure is my name
white as angel wings
embrace me with your love
and keep me there
in your arms
I am forever yours.

Moonlight Dust

A path of magic
the faeries speak in sound
most gentle of beings
a tiny little village
on the way to their place
which is hidden on a secret path
they like to unveil new worlds to wonder
and possibilities
their wings are made of moonlight dust
and shimmer in the dark
they have numerous powers
and are private in their affairs
they like to sleep in flowers
and eat honey all day long
at night they get wild and playful
faeries do exist of that I'm sure
they want us to believe in the unseen
they light your path and ask you to
believe in your own magic.

Dragonfly

I'm working with the faeries
the golden magical ones
they carry all the answers
and have the best insight
they like to work at moonlight
and have little time
they like to speak in riddles
because they love their fun
they love to play with magic
they might even sing you a song
those who can hear them
might answer their call
and for those who can see them
they'll give you their world.

In the Garden

Trees are my friends
and I'm theirs
I walk in the garden
I see my friends
they see me
playing in the garden.

Love in Isolation

A sense of home
of love and beauty
a walk in nature
time in abundance
calm and peaceful
joyful giggles
pure bliss ecstasy
purple clouds
sky on fire
cold and warmth
shared moments
with you
and my loved ones
in the most beautiful garden
that is home.

Twilight

Lovers love the moon
shining in the sky
evening time
going home
on a path
the scent of summer
birds in the air
poets in the making
lovers love to kiss
a kiss a smile
sweet delight of summer.

Wonder

Why does the world have so many trees
and bears in the woods?
why do wolves live in the woods
and not inside my home?
can a book answer me
why the world is so compelling?

The Sky

eyes of wonder and belief
God made the world his
eyes of wonder and belief
God made his world beautifully
eyes of wonder and belief
God made life good and all in it
eyes of wonder and belief
God made us perfectly.

Most Precious Soul

Most precious soul
beneath the sea
the world tumbles
beneath your heart
your kisses speak of love
up above in the sky
the angels sing and pray to God
beneath my heart I find you
softly
lovingly
kissing me.

One Night

One night
the moon was almost full
see me beautiful
the sun comes and warms the cold night away
believe me when I say
the lovers love the world
the lovers know the beauty of love
crystal clear the water is
love is a Cupid's arrow
the lovers know the beauty of love
and the scent of summer.

Love on my Lips

Love permeates the air
the sea is deep
its waters strong
drops of rain
morning shines through
the world is a paradise
sweet child of mine
there are cherries on the trees
and sweet flowers in the grass
the world is beautiful.

Metamorphosis

A drop of turquoise-blue
the sun sets
on a golden leaf
lord of my disguise
you whispered:
"darling never mind
these wings of yours
are the beauties of infinite time
life is a glimpse of the divine."

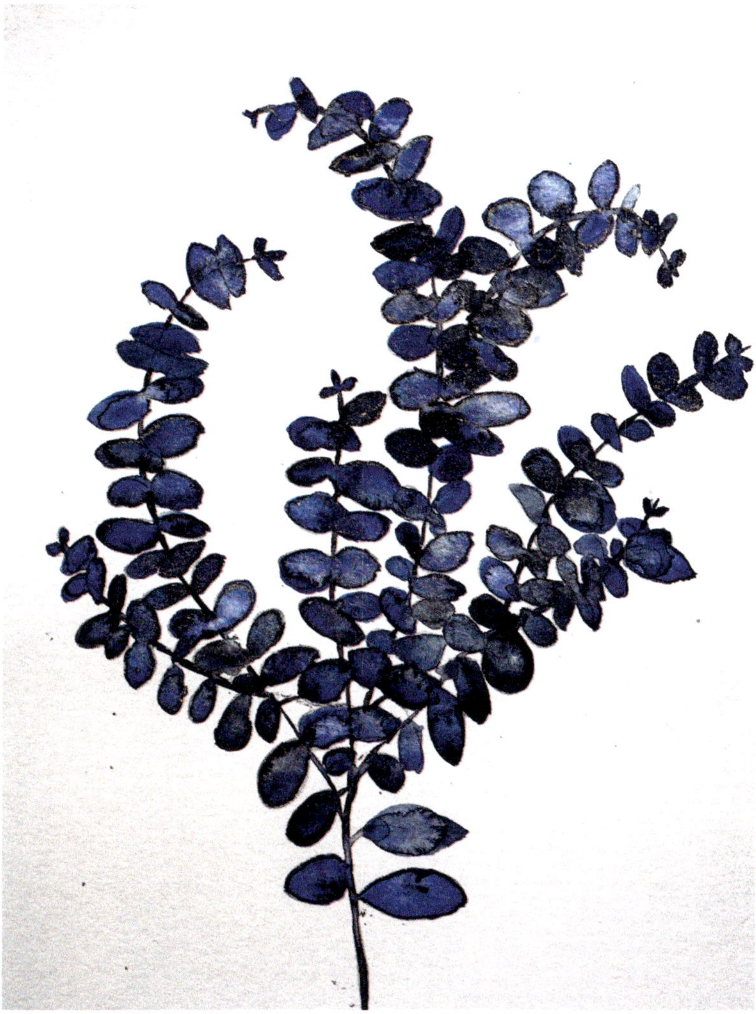

Acknowledgments

I would like to thank Tania Chick for her amazing editorial work on this book, due to her brilliant mind, dedication and co-creative ideas, 'Heartsong' was born in this form. A thanks to Joan Akwue for her design of the book cover and interior.

Photo on back cover by Hailwax Robert
All artwork by Anaïs Giulia
Front Cover - Artwork 'Wild Roses', watercolor on paper, 2020
Back Cover - Artwork 'Crescent Moons', watercolor on paper, 2019
First Chapter - Artwork 'Eukalyptus and Buds", watercolor, 2020
Second Chapter - Artwork 'Summer Bouquet', watercolor on paper, 2020
Third Chapter - Artwork 'Crescent Moons', watercolor on paper, 2019
Acknowledgments - Artwork 'Blue Eukalyptus', watercolor on paper, 2019

Printed in Great Britain
by Amazon